SOCCER

BY KARA L. LAUGHLIN

The Child's World®
childsworld.com

Published by The Child's World®
1980 Lookout Drive • Mankato, MN 56003-1705
800-599-READ • www.childsworld.com

ACKNOWLEDGMENTS
The Child's World®: Mary Swensen, Publishing Director
The Design Lab: Design
Heidi Hogg: Editing
Sarah M. Miller: Editing

PHOTO CREDITS
© anekoho/Shutterstock.com: 16-17, 20-21; anuphadit/
Shutterstock.com: 2-3; Brad Thompson/Shutterstock.com: 13;
Christopher Futcher/iStockphoto.com: 4; Fotokostic/Shutterstock.
com: 19; IS_ImageSource/iStockphoto.com: 15; Laszlo66/
Shutterstock.com: 6-7; Pavel L. Photo and Video/Shutterstock.com:
8-9; SOMKKU/Shutterstock.com: cover, 1; strickke/Shutterstock.
com: 10

ISBN: 9781503807808
LCCN: 2015958219

Printed in the United States of America
Mankato, MN
June, 2016
PA02300

TABLE OF CONTENTS

Game Time!

Are you ready to score some **goals**? Grab some friends and lace up your shoes. Let's play soccer!

Gear

Soccer players need some gear to play. **Cleats** grip the ground. They keep you from slipping. **Shin guards** protect your legs. **Soccer socks** keep your guards in place.

Fast Fact!
More than 250 million people in the world play soccer.

Players

Each team has 11 players. Every player has a job. Some players focus on goals. Others guard the net. All the players work together.

Starting the Game

The **kickoff** starts the game. A player stands in the center of the field. She kicks the ball forward. Then anyone else can kick the ball.

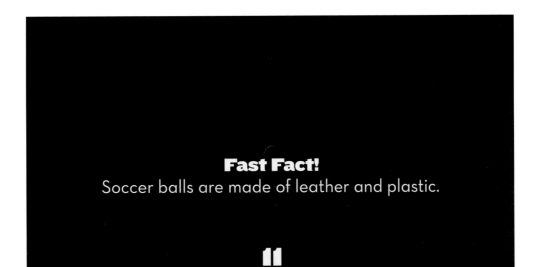

Fast Fact!
Soccer balls are made of leather and plastic.

Moving the Ball

The players **dribble** the ball with their feet. They also **pass** the ball to other players. Sometimes they stop the ball with their chests. The pros even **head** the ball.

Fast Fact!
There are 32 sections on a soccer ball.

No Hands Allowed!

Only the **goalies** can use their hands in soccer. They can grab the ball before it goes in the net. They can throw or kick it to their teammates.

Fast Fact!
Goalies wear gloves that help them grip the ball.

The Field

The soccer field has lines painted in the grass. If a player kicks the ball outside the lines, it is out. The other team gets to throw or kick the ball back in.

Fast Fact!
A soccer field is also called a pitch.

Free Kicks

If someone breaks the rules, the ref may blow her whistle to stop the game. It could mean a **free kick**.

Some players can **bend** the ball on a free kick. They kick the ball so that it curves in the air. This makes it harder for the goalie to catch.

20

Goal! When a team sends the ball into the net, they score a point. Then the other team gets to kick off.

Both teams keep trying to score until time is up. At the end of the game, the team with the most goals wins.

Fast Fact!
The World Cup is the championship for teams all over the world. It is held every four years.

Glossary

bend (BEND): A way to kick the ball so that instead of moving in a straight line, it curves in the air. Players bend the ball to make it harder for the goalies to catch.

cleats (KLEETS): Cleats are special shoes with spikes or knobs on the soles, which help the shoes to grip the turf.

dribble (DRIB-bul): Players dribble by moving the ball with small kicks in order to stay in control of it.

free kick (FREE KIK): A type of kick awarded for some types of fouls. The player gets to shoot close to the goal.

goalies (GOHL-eez): The players who guard the goals to keep the other teams from scoring are the goalies.

goals (GOHLZ): Goals are scored when a soccer ball gets past the goalie and into the net. Goals are worth one point each.

head (HED): Players head the ball when they use their heads to stop or block the ball.

kickoff (KIK-off): A kick that starts play, either at the beginning of the game or after a team scores a goal is called a kickoff.

pass (PAS): Players pass the ball by kicking it to another player.

shin guards (SHIN GARDZ): Shin guards are molded pieces of plastic and foam that are worn on the lower legs for protection from other players' cleats.

soccer socks (SOK-er SOKS): Socks that are made to fit over shin guards and keep them in place are called soccer socks.

To Learn More

In the Library

Crisfield, Deborah W. *The Everything Kids' Soccer Book: Rules, Techniques, and More About Your Favorite Sport!* Avon, MA: Adams Media, 2015.

Hoena, Blake. *National Geographic Kids: Everything Soccer.* Washington, DC: National Geographic Society, 2014.

Nelson, Robin. *From Plastic to Soccer Ball.* Minneapolis, MN: Lerner Publications Company, 2015.

On the Web

Visit our Web site for links about soccer:
childsworld.com/links

Note to Parents, Teachers, and Librarians: We routinely verify our Web links to make sure they are safe and active sites. So encourage your readers to check them out!

Index

About the Author

Kara L. Laughlin is an artist and writer who lives in Virginia with her husband, three kids, two guinea pigs, and a dog. She is the author of two dozen nonfiction books for kids.